DEDICATED TO:

From Cindy
To all readers who are bravely learning to talk about their emotions.
And to my loved ones, who make me feel powerful and strong.

From Nqobile
To my two children, Inioluwa and Ayomikun,
you can handle any emotion, big or small.

www.LilLibros.com

My Mind is a Mountain / Mi mente es una montaña
Published by Little Libros, LLC

Text © 2022 Cindy Montenegro Delgado
Art © 2022 Hycent Nqobile Adigun
Designed by Haydeé Yañez

Library of Congress Control Number 2021946847

Printed in China
Third Edition - 2023   JHP 03/23
27 26 25 24 23   3 4 5

ISBN 978-1-948066-18-1

MY MIND IS A MOUNTAIN

MI MENTE ES UNA MONTAÑA

Written by
CINDY MONTENEGRO

Illustrated by
NQOBILE ADIGUN

Lil' LIBROS

My body is wonderful!
It holds all of my emotions.
Some are small like a mouse,
Others are as big as the ocean.

¡Mi cuerpo es maravilloso!
Contiene muchas emociones.
Algunas son como un ratoncito pequeño,
y otras grandes como el océano.

I have emotions that are easy to show.
Those are fun to have around.
Others can be a little bit tricky,
but they are still important to talk about!

Algunas de mis emociones son fáciles de expresar.
Estas me encantan.
Otras son un poco más difícil,
¡pero aún son importantes de comunicar!

Sometimes I feel happy,
and my mouth smiles from ear to ear.
I skip and I laugh to show others how I feel.

A veces me siento feliz,
y sonrío de oreja a oreja.
Yo salto y me río y demuestro lo que siento.

Sometimes I feel sad and I know this
because my body moves slowly,
I cry and I frown.

A veces me siento triste y mi cuerpo me lo enseña
cuando me muevo lentamente,
lloro y frunzo el ceño.

Sometimes I feel excited and my body does not stay still.
I run and I dance around, exclaiming: YIPPEE!

A veces siento mucha emoción y mi cuerpo no se queda quieto.
Corro y bailo, exclamando: ¡YUPI!

Sometimes I feel angry and I want to scream out loud.
My heart beats fast like a drum, and my feet stomp
on the ground!

A veces siento enojo y quiero gritar muy fuerte.
¡Mi corazón late rápido como un tambor y mis pies pisotean el suelo!

When my emotions get big
and I want to slow them down,
my mind thinks of a quiet place,
where I can sit and breathe.

Cuando mis emociones se hacen grandes
y quiero calmarme,
mi mente piensa en un lugar tranquilo,
donde puedo sentarme y respirar.

I imagine myself on top of a mountain looking at everything down below. From way up here, big things don't seem so big after all!

Me imagino en la cima de una montaña
mirando todo desde arriba.
¡Desde aquí las cosas grandes no parecen
tan grandes después de todo!

My mind is a mountain, powerful and strong.
I can handle every emotion, no matter how big or how small!

Mi mente es una montaña, poderosa y fuerte.
Puedo manejar mis emociones, ¡de tamaño pequeño o grande!

While on my mountain, I sit very still,
my back tall like a tree.
Can you sit very still, and try it with me?

En mi montaña, me siento sin moverme,
con mi espalda alta como un árbol.
¿Puedes tomar asiento para intentarlo conmigo?

I breathe in to smell the flowers: 1...2...3!
I breathe out very slowly, like a gentle breeze.

Respiro profundo para oler las flores: ¡1...2...3!
Con mi boca soplo muy lento, como un suave viento.

Now I feel peaceful, my body is light like a cloud.
I use my words to say what I feel inside,
and that makes me proud.

Ahora siento paz, mi cuerpo ligero como una nube.
Con mis palabras digo lo que siento por dentro,
y eso me enorgullece.

How are you feeling right now?
Who would you like to share your feelings with today?

¿Cómo te sientes en este momento?
¿A quién te gustaría contarle tus sentimientos hoy?

Great job, we did it!
Our strong minds helped us find our way.
We used breathing to handle big emotions,
now we can continue our day.

¡Buen trabajo, lo logramos!
Usamos nuestras mentes fuertes como guía.
Respiramos profundo para manejar grandes emociones,
y ahora podemos continuar con este día.

Your mind is a mountain, powerful and strong.
You can handle every emotion,
no matter how big or how small!

Tu mente es una montaña, poderosa y fuerte.
Puedes manejar tus emociones,
¡de tamaño pequeño o grande!

CINDY MONTENEGRO

I feel so happy to share with you the story of how this book came to life. When I was little, I spent a lot of time outdoors. I got to experience so many beautiful things like listening to the rain fall on my camping tent with my brothers, appreciating the flowers on nature walks with my mom, and looking up at the stars on quiet summer nights with my dad. Taking time to appreciate these things made me feel calm and safe, so whenever I felt big emotions (emotions so big that they felt like they would never go away) it helped to take a deep breath and imagine being surrounded by these peaceful nature scenes. Once I was calm, it was easier to talk about the things that made me feel worried, angry, or sad. My hope is that this book will help every reader be comforted in knowing that their emotions are so important and deserve to be talked about! With all my heart, I hope that this book is also a reminder to caregivers of the important role they play in creating a caring space for their children to express themselves. Wherever in the world this book has found you, I send love from the top of my mountain to yours.

NQOBILE ADIGUN

I thoroughly enjoyed drawing and coloring every page of this book, and my hope is that you will enjoy every one of the illustrations too. This is my first official opportunity to create artwork for a children's book, and I have been honored and humbled by it. Being the illustrator for *My Mind is a Mountain* proved both exhilarating and challenging. Like the character in this beautifully penned story, I too had a range of emotions to deal with; most times I had easier emotions where I was happy and excited, but there were times when tricky emotions kicked in. I am fortunate enough to have an incredible family to speak to when faced with the tricky emotions. And when I had pleasant emotions they were right there with me too. My gratitude for this opportunity is deeper than words can express. May this book, through the words and illustrations, help you to remember that your mind is strong and that you can handle any emotion that comes your way – this now and even when you're a grownup like me.